Footprints

One night a man had a dream. He dreamed he was walking along the beach with the Lord. Across the sky flashed scenes from his life. For each scene, he noticed two sets of footprints in the sand: one belonging to him, and the other to the Lord.

When the last scene of his life flashed before him, he looked back at the footprints in the sand. He noticed that many times along the path of his life there was only one set of footprints. He also noticed that it happened at the very lowest and saddest times in his life.

This really bothered him and he questioned the Lord about it.

"Lord, you said that once I decided to follow you, you'd walk with me all the way. But I have noticed that during the most troublesome times in my life, there is only one set of footprints. I don't understand why when I needed you the most you would leave me."

The Lord replied, "My son, My precious child, I love you and would never leave you. During your times of trial and suffering, when you see only one set of footprints, it was then that I carried you."

Author unknown

THIS BOOK BELONGS TO

Dog the WAG

Dog the WAG

Professor Marvin's Dogged Pursuit
of Canine Words and Phrases

MIKE DARTON

adams
media
AVON, MASSACHUSETTS

Published by Adams Media,
an F+W Publications Company
57 Littlefield Street
Avon, MA 02322
www.adamsmedia.com

Copyright ©2007 Ivy Press Limited
All rights reserved.
ISBN 10: 1-59869-436-7
ISBN 13: 978-1-59869-436-9

Printed and bound in Thailand

This book is available at quantity discounts for bulk purchases.
For information, please call 1-800-289-0963.

A CIP catalog record for this book is available
from the Library of Congress

This book was conceived, designed, and produced by
iBall, an imprint of **Ivy Press**
The Old Candlemakers
West Street, Lewes
East Sussex, BN7 2NZ, UK
www.ivy-group.co.uk

CREATIVE DIRECTOR Peter Bridgewater
PUBLISHER Jason Hook
EDITORIAL DIRECTOR Caroline Earle
ART DIRECTOR Sarah Howerd
SENIOR PROJECT EDITOR Dominique Page
DESIGNER Joanna Clinch
ILLUSTRATOR Joanna Clinch
PHOTOGRAPHER Paul Farnham

J I H G F E D C B A

CONTENTS

Introduction

What was it that the great sage Elvis Presley used to declaim so sonorously? Oh yes: "You ain't nothin' but a hound dog." What he in his wisdom meant, of course, was that "you ain't nothin' if you ain't a hound dog," because, as we all know, dogs are more important than just about anything else in the world. Almost as important as people. That's why the number of doggy words, expressions, and phrases in English is more than ten times greater than the number of words, expressions, and phrases that have to do with any other animal. This book contains a lot of them. Not all of them, because it leaves out (most of) the ones that are just plain *rude*. But you may well be surprised at some that turn out to have strong canine connections.

At the same time, this book is much more than just a list of terms. There are also amazing facts about their linguistic origins and history, about how they came to have the meanings they have, and about how those meanings may or may not have changed over the years. For example, some doggy expressions that are still current in English date (in translation) from the time of ancient Greece and Rome. Linguistically, the Anglo-Saxons bequeathed us the notion of hunting with hounds and keeping them to protect the household. The French-speaking Normans in a similar fashion gave us kennels in which to lodge our pampered canine pets. And from the fifteenth century, genuine English-speakers have also been much given to devising further doggy proverbs and terms. Today's slang, from cockney London through suburban Australia and the southern United States, is meanwhile doggedly keeping us on our toes . . . and giving us paws for thought.

I should, finally, also point out that this invaluable work of canine etymology was compiled under the aegis (that is, the watchful eye and awesome ear) of no less an authority than the sagacious Professor Marvin, dog scholar extraordinary—to whom, indeed, the words "dog scholar" may be applied in so many ways.

A guide to pronunciation symbols

ō   as in bonzo (bón-zō), rose (rōz)
ōō   as in poodle (pōōd'l), pooch (pōōch)
ŏŏ   as in woof (wŏŏf), wolf (wŏŏlf)
ə   as in collar (kóllər), chenille (shə-néel)
ī   as in pile (pīl), fire (fīr)

SYLLABLES
A hyphen indicates syllabic division

STRESS
The mark ´ indicates the stress
on syllables

DOGGY WORDS

POOCH | po͞och |

MEANING: A nondescript household dog, household fleabag

ORIGINS AND HISTORY: Apparently an early twentieth-century term, based on the notion that the household dog may be "stuffed" or overfed (just as things may be stuffed into a *pouch*, and just as *poached* eggs may look swollen and stuffed), with dire consequences for its looks and continued health

This is also one explanation given for the derivation of the word pug, *now defined as "a small, compact dog," but originally a term for a squat elf or hobgoblin alternately known as Pook or Puck. Naturally, no one would ever think of describing an animal of Professor Marvin's noble demeanor and presence as a "pooch."*

BOW-WOW | bów-wów |

MEANING: A dog (as described by a child), doggie

ORIGINS AND HISTORY: Derived in 1576 straight from supposedly childish vocabulary based on the sound of an average medium-pitched dog

French dogs go "wa-wa," and Scandinavian dogs go "how-how." There is just no accounting for the form in which speakers of languages other than English represent the sound of a dog's barking in words. Perhaps they're all deaf. Mind you, even in English, high-pitched dogs may "yap," whereas low-pitched dogs may go "woof."

MUTT | mut |

MEANING: A mongrel, nondescript (allegedly canine) animal, pooch

ORIGINS AND HISTORY: Apparently an abbreviation of a description of someone who is "mutton-headed"—that is, sheep-brained, woolly-minded; no date cited

This is a rare example of a description for humans being transferred to dogs, and not the other way around. But I shouldn't think the sheep are too pleased about it, either.

KENNEL | kénn'l |

MEANING: A plain gable-roofed box or cabin as portable quarters for a dog; doghouse

ORIGINS AND HISTORY: The Norman French, led by William the Conqueror in 1066, brought with them to England the practice of hunting with hounds; in their aristocratic castles, the place where the dogs were kept was known simply as (something like) *canaille*, the "dog-pack," which of course the local Anglo-Saxons who were employed as servants quickly converted to *kennel*, regarding it as a term for the animals' quarters rather than for the animals themselves

The difference in meaning between the aristocratic (Latin–French) kennel *and the plain and usually pejorative (Germanic)* doghouse *has thus persisted in English for close on a thousand years.*

LITTER | líttər |

MEANING: A brood of pups: the puppies born all at the same time

ORIGINS AND HISTORY: Another example of an aristocratic Norman French word (*litière*, "place for lying in," from medieval Latin *lectaria*) that was slightly misunderstood by the Anglo-Saxon servants in England toward the end of the eleventh century; for one thing, the Anglo-Saxon "place for lying in" was a bed made with straw padding, so whereas the French-speaking nobility regarded a "litter" as a portable couch, the Old English "litter" became the bedstraw used not just for lying in, but primarily for a *lying-in*—a birth—and then for the animals (especially, in those days, piglets) born in it

The straw on which the birth took place naturally became pretty dirty during the event and had to be thrown away afterward—and that is how "litter" came also to mean "trash discarded and left lying around."

DOGFIGHT | dóg-fīt |

MEANING: A fight in which combatants continually seek some positional advantage before attempting a final vicious and decisive lunge

ORIGINS AND HISTORY: Evidently based on the way dogs actually spar for dominance, often by apparently chasing each other's tails, the term originated from the time of World War I (1915) and was used for decades primarily to describe close-range combat between military aircraft

The term may have been influenced by the medieval English expression "to fight dog" (also "to fight bear"), meaning to go on fighting until there is one clear victor—but the transference to military aircraft is easily explainable in that airplanes also have tails that can be chased.

SNAP | snap |

MEANING: Sudden closure of the jaws (especially by a dog)—thus any sudden movement, thus anything particularly sudden

ORIGINS AND HISTORY: Originally (1490s), the snapping shut of the jaws of a dog—which is why the overall dentition and oral volume of a dog is still technically known as its "snap"

Whereas English has concentrated on the suddenness of a "snap," other Germanic languages, in using the same word, have retained the notion of a "quick mouthful." So Germans drink Schnapps—*strong drink of which only a mouthful can be swallowed at a time. And the Dutch like to* snoep *—eat small snacks in secret (although the English variant of this word,* snoop, *has come to mean to try to find out other people's secrets in general). Incidentally, this shows that the word* snack *itself derives (1680s for liquids, 1730s for food) as a dialectal variant of* snap.

DOG-EARED | dóg-eerd |

MEANING: Folded over, creased, crumpled

ORIGINS AND HISTORY: First recorded in 1659 to describe a well-thumbed book that had "dog's ears"—that is, pages in which the top corner had been folded back

The triangular flaps of book pages with the corner turned over do look like the flappy ears of some dogs. Professor Marvin can't understand why the expression is considered mildly derogatory, but will turn a deaf ear.

DOGPILE | dóg-pīl |

MEANING: A mass tackle on a single player, a forceful pouncing by several people on one other person

ORIGINS AND HISTORY: Term first used in football as the name of a ploy involving the tackling by a number of defensive players of a single offensive player; because for some teams the instruction for this ploy was the one word "dogpile," the term became used both as a description of a maul or scrimmage centering on a single person and as a general invitation to anybody present to join in the assault

The expression is apocryphally said to originate from a Bugs Bunny "biographical" cartoon movie sequence in which he is being chased by a group of dogs, who all leap on him together. But, perhaps more significantly, the word has since also become a term for the instant hostile response of a group of respondents to a naive (or stupid) Internet research request for information—and has subsequently become the name of an independent Internet search engine.

BARK | bark |

MEANING: The sound a dog makes

ORIGINS AND HISTORY: The word comes directly from Anglo-Saxon *beorc* and initially applied only to dogs, apparently representing the sound made; by Geoffrey Chaucer's time (late 1300s), however, the word—in the most usual form, *berk*—could be applied figuratively also to human vocalizations

Anything that barks is a barker. But from around 1700, a "barker" was a term for someone who stood outside a store or a box office and urged people to enter and spend their money: some traveling circuses and funfairs still employ them. By the early 1800s, a "barker" was also a slang term for a pistol, as mentioned by Sir Walter Scott and (half a generation later) by Charles Dickens. Neither, however, described the use of a barker to shoot a barker.

Woof

WOOF, WOOF-WOOF | woŏf | woŏf-woŏf|

MEANING: The supposed sound of a low-pitched bark; by transference, a dog (as described by a child), doggie

ORIGINS AND HISTORY: First recorded as both noun and verb in 1804—almost 230 years after "bow-wow" and 136 years after "yap"

....

YAPPY | yapi |

MEANING: Tending to bark shrilly; barking persistently at a high pitch

ORIGINS AND HISTORY: The verb "to yap" dates in print from 1668 and is said to have originated simply as a representation of the sound

....

SNARL | snarl |

MEANING: To make a sound like a dog baring its teeth and growling

ORIGINS AND HISTORY: First recorded in modern English in 1589, apparently as an adaptation of an earlier *snarr*, closely akin to *sneer* and *snore* (and to the extension of the latter, *snort*)—all suggestive of facial movement accompanied by less-than-peaceable sound effects

FIDO | fīdō |

MEANING: A classic and now ludicrously old-fashioned name for a household dog

ORIGINS AND HISTORY: The Latin word *fidus* means "trusty" or "faithful." In its later Italian form *fido* was, sentimentally, applied as a name for dogs in aristocratic houses in the English-speaking world toward the end of the eighteenth century

Probably the most famous owner of a dog named Fido was President Abraham Lincoln—although that may say more about him than about what he expected of the animal...

BONZO | bón-zō |

MEANING: An old-fashioned and now ridiculous name for a household dog

ORIGINS AND HISTORY: The creation of cartoonist George Studdy, Bonzo the pudgy terrier pup appeared in *The Sketch* magazine—published in London, England, from 1922 to 1927—and was one of the first cartoon characters to become popular worldwide; he featured on posters and postcards, in books, on ashtrays, in jigsaw puzzles, as a vehicle mascot, and (despite what would now be considered a distinctly rugged appearance) as a cuddly toy

This pet name was not always applied to dogs. The Bonzo with whom Ronald Reagan starred (Bedtime for Bonzo, 1951) was in fact a chimp.

REX | reks |

MEANING: Ruler, king; but Rex is also a personal name

ORIGINS AND HISTORY: Latin for "ruler," "king," and the root of such English words as *regal, reign, regulate,* and *rector*

As a name for a dog, Rex was popularized in the early twentieth century in a series of silent movies entitled Rex, The Wonder Dog—a title that was used again by DC Comics for a comic series between 1952 and 1959. Though still used as a dog's name, Rex is now generally regarded as outmoded to the point of being slightly dull.

PUP, PUPPY | pup | púppi |

MEANING: A newborn dog, very young dog

ORIGINS AND HISTORY: The first form of the word in English was *puppy*, apparently borrowed in the late 1580s from the French *poupée*, "doll," "plaything," and thus "pet"; *pup* is a later (1770s) abbreviation, although the verb "to pup" is recorded a little earlier

Before the 1580s, the usual word for a puppy was whelp, *from the Anglo-Saxon* hwelp. *It may or may not be a coincidence that the young pet dog of Mary, Queen of Scots—who was executed in England in 1587 by order of Queen Elizabeth I, and whose first language was French, since she had been raised in France—was nationally famous for having run out from beneath her skirts at the site of Mary's execution. Meanwhile, the only other animal whose young is currently and ordinarily known as a pup is the seal (and sea lion)—although this usage dates only from the 1850s and is presumably based on the seal pup's appealing round eyes and snubby bewhiskered nose, reminiscent of many a newborn dog's.*

WHELP | welp |

MEANING: An undomesticated young dog, wild cub

ORIGINS AND HISTORY: The ordinary word for a puppy until the 1580s, it had to change its meaning slightly once the word *puppy* took over

Unless unexpectedly rehabilitated, whelp is a word that will soon be found only in crosswords, Scrabble dictionaries and the Authorized (King James) Version of the Bible—in which, remarkably, it refers to the offspring either of a lion (Ezekiel 19:2, 3, 5; Nahum 2:12) or of a bear (2 Samuel 17:8; Proverbs 17:12; Hosea 13:8). Such associations do not, however, contribute to explaining its etymology, which remains stubbornly obscure—although they do indicate that originally the word did not necessarily have anything to do with dogs, but concerned the young of mammals known to be fearsome in teeth and paw. This makes nonsense of the claim by many linguistic commentators that it derives as a sort of combination of wail, howl, and yelp—all suggestive of sound.

HELLHOUND | hél-hownd |

MEANING: A dog of hell, thus either a fearsome watchdog at the gate of hell (such as the mythical Cerberus) or a slavering hound ready, at the command of demons or the Devil, to increase the torments of those sinners dispatched to hell on the Last Day

ORIGINS AND HISTORY: Rather surprisingly, these two meanings are precisely those of *helle hund* in Old English (Anglo-Saxon), including the specific reference to Cerberus; it was not until early medieval times that the expression could be used to describe a person of fiendish characteristics

In Shakespeare's King Richard III, *Richard's mother is told: "From forth the kennel of thy womb has crept a hell-hound that doth hunt us all to death"—an extension of the original idea that, in yet another way, was later taken up by Arthur Conan Doyle in the Sherlock Holmes story* The Hound of the Baskervilles.

JACKAL | jáckawl |

MEANING: A wild dog of the true dog genus *Canis*, that is found in southern Asia, southern Europe, and northern Africa; a scavenger and sometimes a pack predator, with an unpleasant reputation

ORIGINS AND HISTORY: Jackals have been renowned since ancient times for preying on the carcasses of mammals, including humans; the word *jackal* probably derives in English from Old Persian *shagal*, itself in turn a variant of Sanskrit *srgal*, which may mean "scratcher" or "cryer"

In human mythology, jackals are associated strongly with the dead and the afterworld—because they are so interested in corpses. That was why the ancient Egyptian conductor of human souls to the judge of the dead was the jackalheaded Anubis. Indeed, as the introducer of souls to the Underworld, he may have represented the dog Cerberus, guardian of the ancient Greek portal of hell—and the Sanskrit srgal, *or "jackal," may be a variant of that same name.*

MONGREL | múng-grəl |

MEANING: A dog of unknown and evidently mixed parentage

ORIGINS AND HISTORY: First recorded in 1486 as *mengrell*, deriving from the verb *meng*, meaning "to produce by mixing," related to the modern words *mingle* and *among*

The spelling was still fluid in Shakespeare's time at the very beginning of the seventeenth century—unless he was going through a particularly dyslexic phase when in King Lear *he made Kent describe Oswald as "the Sonne and Heire of a Mungrill Bitch" . . . among other things.*

BITZER | bit-súr |

MEANING: A mongrel, dog of unfathomably mixed ancestry

ORIGINS AND HISTORY: English schoolboy joke of the 1940s through 1960s, in which the family dog is described as a "bitzer" because its pedigree combines "bitzer this and bitzer that"

CUR | kur |

MEANING: A dog of unknown background, but even more significantly, of unpleasant and potentially threatening demeanor

ORIGINS AND HISTORY: Said to have originated from around 1220 and to be based on the sound of growling—"Grrr . . ." The initial recorded version of the word is as a prefix in the medieval English *kurdogge* (in which the syllable *kur-* relates to Old Norse *kurra*, "to growl"). This would make more sense than trying to relate the term to Norman French expressions, from which English has derived such words as *occur* and *recur*, in which the element *-cur* has to do with "running (in a course or on a path)." To the Norman French, dogs were not runners but hunters; it also fits with the fact that English *cur* might through Old Norse therefore be cognate with Finnish *koira*, "dog"

Shakespeare certainly recognized a difference between a dog and a cur—the cur being the less presentable in polite society. In The Two Gentlemen of Verona, *the servant Launce is asked by his master Proteus what Mistress Silvia's reaction was to Proteus' gift to her of a dog. Launce replies: "Marry, she says your dog was a cur and tells you currish thanks is good enough for such a present." It turns out that Launce has substituted a different animal, and his interview with the angry Proteus is thereupon cut short—or cur-tailed.*

CYNIC | sínnik |

MEANING: A person who does not believe in the natural goodness of humankind, and who thus tends to sneer at or be sardonic about anything that suggests altruism or selfless kindness by one person toward another

ORIGINS AND HISTORY: Comes from the name of a school of philosophers (*Kunikoi*, "the Cynics") established in ancient Greece in around 400 BCE. The name was not intended to be particularly complimentary, because *kunikos* is the adjective derived from *kuōn* "dog," suggesting that the members of the school were forever snarling at well-meaning people "like dogs." The name was nonetheless accepted by members of the school, who thereafter felt no compunction about pressing their beliefs in a fairly aggressive way upon all and sundry

The main teaching of the Cynics was that virtue and self-control are their own rewards in life and should be regarded as the primary source of happiness.

CYNOSURE | sīnə-shoor |

MEANING: The center of attention, the star attraction, the magnetic draw

ORIGINS AND HISTORY: An ancient Greek astronomical reference to the Pole Star, the star that marks the north in the night sky and that in former centuries was accordingly a primary directional indicator to sailors. From a modern viewpoint, that star—Polaris—is the final star in the constellation Ursa Minor, the Lesser Bear, but to the Greeks the whole constellation formed one end of their much bigger version of what the Romans slightly later called Canis Major, the Great Dog. This essential guiding light for navigators was thus the very tip of the tail of the Dog: *kunos oura*, "Dog's tail"—the cynosure

The fact that at least one of the two bears in the nighttime sky (Ursa Major and Ursa Minor) was "overlapped" by at least one of the two dogs (Canis Major and Canis Minor) may have given rise to the myth of the hunter Actaeon torn to pieces by his own hounds at the command of Artemis, who was surprised while bathing. Despite later being identified by the Romans with their moon goddess Diana, Artemis to the early Greeks was the Mother Bear, Ursa Major, and would have taken seriously any threat by Actaeon's (Orion's) dogs toward her cub Ursa Minor.

CANAILLE | kə-nī |

MEANING: Rabble, mob, riffraff

ORIGINS AND HISTORY: A French loan-word, but ultimately derived from Italian *canaglia* "pack of dogs." First included in a printed work in English in 1676, but apparently evidenced in esoteric conversation at least sixty years earlier

Whoever it was in 1676 who decided to import the trendy French—Italian word canaille *into English probably didn't realize he was actually only reintroducing the word* kennel *in a different sense.*

MUZZLE | múzz'l |

MEANING: The external mouthparts of a dog; also a device intended to partly cover those mouthparts in order to prevent aggressive use of the teeth, and generally clipped additionally over the nose

ORIGINS AND HISTORY: The word's derivation is unknown; commentators have suggested an Old French verb meaning essentially "to put one's head back and raise one's mouth"—either to sing (as in "music") or just to contemplate (as in "muse")

The term is often used figuratively of an attempt to stifle speech (as with a gag), although that arises technically as something of a confusion with muffle.

DOGSBODY | dógz-boddi |

MEANING: A person required to do all the menial tasks; gofer, grunt, drudge

ORIGINS AND HISTORY: British Royal Navy early nineteenth-century slang for the lumpy gray-white mass that was a standard meal for the ordinary sailors, and was prepared by boiling dried (gray) peas in a muslin bag. Evidently the lowly class of sailor who fed regularly on this slop was one who might be ordered to do anything menial that needed doing—but it was not until the early twentieth century that midshipmen and junior officers who found themselves doing the menial chores that the senior officers did not want to take on began in turn to describe themselves as "dogsbodies"

(DOG) LEAD | (dóg) léed |

MEANING: The strap between dog owner and dog collar when out walking in public; some have devices that facilitate tensioning and slackening, for the purposes of training the dog

ORIGINS AND HISTORY: Whereas a "leash" by etymology is something that is quite *loose* around the dog's neck, the word *lead* derives from ancient Germanic verbal elements that mean "to cause to go" and thus imply pressure

The intention of a dog lead is evidently for the human to lead the dog. Few dogs seem to appreciate this, however. Most are happier to run ahead, acting as an individual dog team towing the human behind.

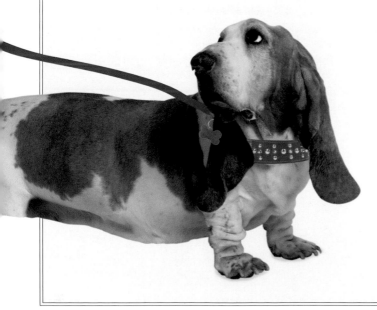

DOGTROT | dóg-trot |

MEANING: The easy, loping speed at which a dog normally accompanies a fast-walking human (assuming that the dog is not of gigantic proportions and the human not minuscule)

ORIGINS AND HISTORY: Naturally derives partly from the verb "to trot," which comes from Middle English as a frequentative of *tread*—but the compound noun *dogtrot* dates only from 1664

A dogtrot house is a form of dual log cabin traditional to the southeastern United States: it has a porch on two opposite sides, a chimney at each end, and a connecting (sometimes open) passageway in the center between its otherwise separate halves. Its design is peculiarly successful in providing ventilation during hot and humid summers. Occupants' dogs tended to travel at a dogtrot between one end and the other.

TERRIER | térri-ər |

MEANING: Various breeds of small, intelligent, and courageous dogs; someone who perseveres when striving to reach a goal

ORIGINS AND HISTORY: The dogs were originally bred by Norman French aristocrats in twelfth-century England to assist hunters by chasing burrowing animals (such as foxes, rabbits, and stoats) into and out of their burrows underground; in Norman French they were *chiens terriers*, "dogs of the earth"

Norman French terrier *referred to "earth" not only as soil, but as the underground lair of the burrowing animal (in the way that a fox still makes its home in an "earth") To flush animals out of their burrow might take a dog some considerable time and effort, and accordingly one of the main implications of the word* terrier *in English today is that of persistence.*

TYKE | tīk |

MEANING: A non-pedigree and less than well-trained dog; persistently troublesome terrier; mischievous or bumptious person (especially a child)

ORIGINS AND HISTORY: Old Scandinavian *tīk* meant a dog that was likely to cause problems, thus particularly a bitch. U.S. English has concentrated since the seventeenth century on the more canine aspects, whereas British English has concentrated on the unruliness, especially as applied (from 1700) to people from Yorkshire or Scotland

In the 1850s, the kind of thief who hung around outside wealthier homes hoping to steal the household dogs—often so as to return them later for a reward—when not described as a "dog-nipper" was known as a "tike-lurker."

ROVER | rṓvər |

MEANING: One who roves or wanders—the classic name for a dog for at least thirty years from the 1920s

ORIGINS AND HISTORY: To "rove" was apparently coined with its current meaning in around 1536; however, by 1607 it had become an archery term, and to "rove" was to shoot at a randomly selected target (which might therefore be in any direction and at any distance). Within another hundred years it had retrieved its original meaning, thanks to confusion with the Dutch term *rover*, meaning "robber" and especially "pirate," and sea rovers were then held not only to rob, but also to wander the oceans at will

DOG-WHISTLE | dóg-wiss'l |

MEANING: A description by political commentators of announcements by political leaders intended to alert subordinates and allies to themes and policies that are about to be emphasized or publicized, without simultaneously alerting political opponents or members of the media

ORIGINS AND HISTORY: The dog-whistle, which was invented by Sir Francis Galton (1822–1911), typically emits sound between 16,000 and 22,000 Hertz—of which only the range 16,000–20,000 Hertz is audible to the human ear in children up to about the age of 11. After the age of 11, the range of human hearing decreases rapidly, and by middle age the top of the range is usually about 14,000 Hertz

It is because the dog-whistle is, with reason, sometimes alternately called the "silent whistle" that it has come to have its political connotations.

....

BERRYHUCKLE | bérri-huck'l |

MEANING: A round of drinks (in Scotland)

ORIGINS AND HISTORY: Coined in recent times as a deliberate distortion on top of rhyming slang: "Huckleberry Hound" implies "round" (of drinks), and "Huckleberry" is then reversed—and not Spoonerized, as claimed by some commentators—to "berryhuckle"

CHENILLE | shə-néel |

MEANING: A sort of velvety cord made up of a central thread from which "hairs" of silk or wool hang relatively loosely, used to trim or border robes and dresses

ORIGINS AND HISTORY: An eighteenth-century French word for a type of hairy caterpillar—yet ultimately derived from the Latin *canicula*, "little (female) dog"

What is even more extraordinary is that the word caterpillar *itself derives from Latin words meaning "hairy cat."*

DOG-FENNEL, DOG-GRASS | dóg-fénn'l | dóg-graass |

MEANING: Alternative names for various plants

ORIGINS AND HISTORY: The plants were nominally associated with dogs mostly because they were once regarded as "poorer" versions of other similar plants, and thus were supposedly more suited to dogs than to humans; dog-fennel (*Aster ericoides*, heath aster, or *Matricaria* species, mayweed) is in this way not "real" fennel, and dog-grass (*Triticum repens* or *T. caninum*, also called dog wheat and couch grass) is likewise not "real" grass

*Other examples of this renaming of plants include the dog cabbage (*Thelygonum cynocrambe, *a Mediterranean herb), and the dog parsley (*Aethusa cynapium, *also known as fool's parsley or lesser hemlock). That they have been associated in folk memory with dogs for at least a couple of centuries is evident in their latin names, which include the Greek element *cyn-, *"dog."*

DOG-ROSE | dóg-rōz |

MEANING: A species of wild rose

ORIGINS AND HISTORY: The association of this plant with dogs goes back to ancient Greece, where it was known as the *kuno-rhodon*, and thereafter in the Latin of ancient Rome as *cynorrodon*—"dog rose"; by medieval times, it was known as *Rosa canina*, and toward the end of the sixteenth century this had been translated into English as "dog-rose"; alternative names include brier rose and wild brier

It is possible that even in the days of ancient Greece and Rome the dog-rose—growing, as it did, wild and in hedges—was regarded as somehow a poor relation to the cultivated rose, although the cultivation of roses was virtually unknown at the time. More likely, the rose hips that are the fruit of the wild rose were perceived to be the kind of fruit that dogs might eat, because they could not be consumed by humans without considerable preparation. Adequately prepared, however, rose hips have many medicinal properties valuable to humans—both as an astringent and a diuretic—and by weight they contain up to fifty times the quantity of vitamin C found in an orange.

ROTTWEILER | rót-wīlər |

MEANING: A type of dog first bred in the German town of Rottweil

ORIGINS AND HISTORY: Rottweil means "red village," but for all its obviously straightforward German name, it is in fact the oldest town in southwestern Germany, founded as an urban center by the Romans in 73 CE—although inhabitants had lived there on and off from at least a thousand years earlier

The dog was originally a Roman cattle-herding dog—Rottweil was on the cattle-drove path to the major city of Württemberg—and was formally known as the Rottweiler metzgershund, *"the butchers' dog of Rottweil." A decade before World War I, the Rottweiler became the unofficial breed of the police and the standard guard dog in Germany.*

DOBERMAN, DOBERMANN | dṓbər-mən |

MEANING: A type of dog crossbred for specific purposes

ORIGINS AND HISTORY: Ludwig Dobermann was a tax collector and therefore beloved by all his neighbors in Apolda, near Weimar in Thuringia—so much so that he thought it necessary to breed a special type of dog to defend him against those who, for one reason or another, did not feel all that neighborly toward him. He eventually, in the 1860s to 1880s, bred the Doberman pinscher

Pinscher is the German for "terrier," and is said literally to mean "biter" or "nipper." There are several pinschers other than the Doberman, notably the German, the Austrian, and the miniature. The German pinscher was one of the breeds combined by Herr Dobermann to create his own guard dog; others were the German shepherd, the Rottweiler, and the Manchester terrier. With such a genetic background, Dobermans require firm training from a very early age. I believe in firm training. I began with Professor Marvin when he was at an early age, too. Unhappily, Professor Marvin seems to interpret all the various instructions I have tried to teach him in one of only three ways: "Do nothing different from what you are doing," "Make yourself even more comfortable, if you can find a way of doing so," and "Please ignore everything I say."

LURCHER | lúrchər |

MEANING: A crossbred dog (traditionally a cross between a collie and a greyhound or deerhound) that was much used by poachers in England in the mid-1600s to catch hares and rabbits

ORIGINS AND HISTORY: The name derives from the same origin as *lurker*, and thus conveniently describes both dog and poacher as one who "lurks" or prowls, hoping to take nefarious advantage of whatever eventuates—especially where some form of theft might be involved

If the dog was distracted while operating on the poacher's behalf, or just decided to run off and forget the mission altogether, the poacher might be said to have been "left in the lurch" by the dog. But the most surprising thing about the word lurch *is that the meaning we think of now as the ordinary one—"to falter and drop suddenly to one side"—is in fact a relatively new meaning introduced as mariners' slang in the 1850s.*

BOXER | bóksər |

MEANING: A type of dog originally bred in Germany for baiting bulls

ORIGINS AND HISTORY: Although the breed originated in Germany in the 1850s, it was not until the 1930s that it received its English name, when it was first seen at Cruft's Dog Show in London. It was given that name specifically because of its pugnacious look and because, when excited, it tends to rear on its hind legs and wave its forepaws in front of itself

In fact, maybe they didn't call it a kangaroo only because the kangaroo had been named (in English) 160 years earlier. Nonetheless, despite its ferocious snub-nosed countenance and its naturally boisterous behavior, this is a dog that in some countries is trusted to such an extent as to be a guide dog for blind and otherwise disabled humans.

WHINE | wīn |

MEANING: A nasal wail; an intoned moan of complaint

ORIGINS AND HISTORY: The original Anglo-Saxon word (*hwín*) is intended as a representation of a sound—the sound of an arrow whizzing or whistling through the air—but by 1400 the word was applied instead to vocalization by humans and (particularly) by dogs, in the same rising and falling manner

A modern derivative of the same original Anglo-Saxon word is what Americans think of as a British word, but the British think of as an Australian verb—whinge, meaning "to complain persistently and childishly."

UNDERDOG | úndər-dog |

MEANING: Someone perceived, rightly or wrongly, to be at a disadvantage; a likely loser or also-ran, who nonetheless has a mathematical chance of winning

ORIGINS AND HISTORY: A U.S. expression dating from 1887, but at that time referring specifically to the loser of a dogfight

In some English-speaking areas of the world the underdog is not the bottom dog—just a dog that is beneath the top dog and who may in due course, one way or another, take over the top dog's position. In the United States, however, the underdog may alternately be described as the bottom dog, and thus as the total opposite of the top dog. Despite other suggestions notably, that the top and bottom dogs were the two men engaged in sawing a plank with a two-handed saw in a sawpit—all these expressions derive from descriptions of dogfights.

WOLF | wŏŏlf |

MEANING: The fiercest, wildest dog of the northern hemisphere

ORIGINS AND HISTORY: In English the word derives from Germanic sources, but it has cognates in most other Indo-European languages, although many are so unrecognizable as to make the original meaning obscure

It is interesting that in some cultures it was not how the wolf ate that was so striking, but how much the wolf ate. A little girl wearing a red riding-hood would after all have been but a casual snack—a mere mouthful—to a wolf dressed up in grandma's best, let alone in sheep's clothing. That is why we can talk about "wolfing" our food down, and why "keeping the wolf from the door" can mean "having enough to eat."

LUPUS | loō-pəss |

MEANING: Any one of a number of specific skin diseases that cause deep scarring, with or without patchy discoloration and deformation of the underlying tissues

ORIGINS AND HISTORY: A condition (actually a sign pertaining to several different conditions) first described by English medical authorities in around 1590, which is why it is in Latin; it means "wolf"—apparently with reference to the depth and disfigurement of the scarring, as if caused by a wolf's canine teeth

The patchy discoloration may well also have influenced the choice of Latin name, in that wild dogs (especially wolves and foxes) in medieval England tended to be afflicted with mange, causing bald spots. This is how the relatively common scalp condition alopecia (Greek alopex, "fox") came to be so called—and Greek alopex is etymologically cognate with Latin lupus. Meanwhile, the Greek for "wolf" was lukos (lycos), and another human medical condition associated with wolves is lycanthropy, a psychological state in which a person firmly believes he or she is a wolf. This is the origin of the werewolf (in which the first element were-corresponds to Anglo-Saxon wer, "man" or "person," cognate with Latin vir).

FOGDOG | fóg-dog |

MEANING: A brief gap in a sea mist; a clear spot in otherwise thick fog

ORIGINS AND HISTORY: A relatively modern term, apparently based on the notion that such gaps or clear spaces accompany larger patches of fog, in the same way that dogs accompany humans

SUNDOG | sún-dog |

MEANING: A "mock sun," a sort of optical halo that distorts the apparent shape of the sun, generally when it is fairly low in a bright sky with high cloud cover

ORIGINS AND HISTORY: Evidently a dialectal term for a sea haze or light mist, as used by Florida fisher folk, before physicists got hold of it and added the refractive properties that now characterize it

Sundogs, for which the technical term is parhelia, *are caused by light interference through plate crystals descending horizontally from the clouds. They may be iridescently colored or transparent with bright edges, depending on the observer's viewpoint.*

DOGFISH | dóg-fish |

MEANING: Any of various small sharks, mostly resident in offshore waters of the northern Atlantic Ocean

ORIGINS AND HISTORY: Apparently so called because to deep-sea fishermen they were of less value than "real" fish. The word was first recorded in 1475

The fishermen were partly right: sharks are, after all, not "real" fish, but primitive species that do not have a proper bony skeleton. The name is also applied to other marine species that are not "real" fish [see mud puppy, *page 88].*

DOGGER | dógg^r |

MEANING: A medieval two-masted Dutch fishing boat

ORIGINS AND HISTORY: The word is medieval Dutch and is said to have meant "cod fisher," for the boats were specifically intended to trawl for cod

Yet the boats themselves were strangely flat-bowed, pushing squarely forward into the waves like a bluff bulldog . . . and although the Dutch for "dog" is hond, *dog in Dutch means "bulldog." Such ships with bulldog bows might reasonably therefore be called (bull)doggers.*

DOGWOOD | dóg-wŏod |

MEANING: Any one of the shrubs and trees of the family *Cornaceae*, but especially those of the subgenus *Swida* (or Dogwood *Cornus*), of which the berries are to some degree toxic to humans

ORIGINS AND HISTORY: According to most etymologists, the dogwood is so called only because it bears dogberries, in which the element "dog" implies "not suitable for human consumption"; other etymologies have been suggested, but do not stand up to rigorous scientific scrutiny

The dogwood (ironically Cornus florida*) is the state tree and flower of the Commonwealth of Virginia in the United States, and (as* Cornus nuttallii*) the provincial flower of British Columbia in Canada. A cold snap between mid-April and mid-May may be described as a "dogwood winter" because that is the time when the dogwood blooms.*

FIREDOGS | fïr-dog |

MEANING: Metal stands intended to support burning logs in a home fireplace; in many northern areas of the United States, firedogs are better known as "andirons"

ORIGINS AND HISTORY: Apparently coined sometime between 1828 and 1913, probably in the southern United States; the expression has since traveled all around the world—but no one knows why they should be "dogs"

It is surprising how common the combination of fire and dogs is, around the world, although interpretations are wildly different. January 29, 2006, for example, was the beginning of the Year of the Fire Dog, according to the Chinese calendar . . . but that is a specifically astrological creature: a real dog of a kind, but categorized as an alternative to a wood dog, a metal dog, an earth dog, and a water dog. Yet another type of fire dog—and this time a real live dog—is the sort of dog trained by local fire departments in the United States to assist in anything from arson investigation through crowd control.

SPANIEL | spán-yəl |

MEANING: A type of small to medium-sized dog that has long, silky hair and drooping ears, a keen sense of smell, and a liking for human company

ORIGINS AND HISTORY: The Norman French conquerors of England in 1066 brought with them dogs they reckoned to have imported from Spain, and therefore described them as *espaigneul*, or "Spanish"

In one of the first-ever tirades on behalf of feminism, at the end of the fourteenth century, Chaucer has the Wife of Bath (Wife of Bath's Prologue, line 273) turn roundly on another Canterbury pilgrim and berate him for suggesting that a woman might be no more than a "spaynel" who leaps on a man and fawns on him until she gets what she wants. Regrettably, this was to be a primary context of the word for at least the next two centuries.

BIRD-DOG | búrd-dog |

MEANING: To try to find out in advance all that can be discovered (on a subject, particularly on a proposed project); to track down information that may be useful to oneself or to others

ORIGINS AND HISTORY: U.S. expression that derives from hunting game birds, using a dog first to find the birds, then to set them up for the hunter to shoot

By the 1930s this verb had taken on additional slang meanings, mostly to do with spotting criminal (or at least dishonest) opportunities for easy pickings.

SETTER | séttər |

MEANING: A type of dog trained to flush game birds out of the undergrowth and then sit still (remain "set") while the hunter with the crossbow or shotgun fired away; it remained ready to retrieve any birds shot

ORIGINS AND HISTORY: First applied mainly to a variety of spaniel, the term was later (from 1576) technically restricted to any of three specific breed varieties then called "setters"

The sporting connection and the original threefold action are retained in English in the track athlete's starting orders: ready, get set, go!

HACKLES | háck'lz |

MEANING: The sharp, spiky hairs along the neck and back of a dog, which may become prominent in times of anticipation or excitement

ORIGINS AND HISTORY: "Hackles" are little "hacks," and "hacks" are rough, spiky edges as might be created and left by the operation of a hacksaw or a rough comb when combing flax (for which the technical term is precisely "hackling")

To raise hackles *is to rouse either to a state of anxiety or to resentment or anger. And that is what* heckling *a speaker can do, too—which is not so surprising, since* hackle *and* heckle *are cognate words.*

....

FANG | fang |

MEANING: A sharp and prominent tooth, a canine's canine

ORIGINS AND HISTORY: A Germanic word deriving from a verb meaning "to seize," "to keep hold of" (modern German *fangen*, Dutch *vangen*, "to catch," "to capture")

Fangs were thus teeth for grasping prey with and for preventing them from getting away. One derivative in Dutch is the word gevangenis, *"jail."*

GROWL | growl |

MEANING: A continuous low-pitched snarling sound (especially one emanating from an unfriendly dog), a menacing rumble

ORIGINS AND HISTORY: Probably an extension of the sound "Grrr" and therefore an equivalent of similar words like *groan, grumble, grouch, grouse, gripe,* and *grump* (some of which have cognates in other Indo-European languages)—[see also *cur*, page 27]

Anything that growls is a growler—and, far from suggesting any reason to complain, growler is a traditional American word for an airtight glass container of a half-gallon of locally brewed beer. In this context, however, the term originated before the use of glass containers — in fact when the beer was instead transported in semi-sealed galvanized pails (1880s–1910s) Because the seals were not totally airtight, gas from the beer sometimes used to escape during transportation, and it has been suggested that the result was a sort of growling sound—hence the name.

DOG-COLLAR | dóg-kollər |

MEANING: A collar for a dog, but by extension also the stiff white collar worn by some clergymen and women, a choker or necklet (most often of a plain or flattish design), and a chain or string worn loosely around the neck from which dog tags with identification and other personal information are suspended [see *dog tag*, page 98]

ORIGINS AND HISTORY: It ought to be obvious that the collar for a dog is in fact rarely like any of the other collars listed above: part of the purpose of a canine's collar, after all, may be to assist in training the dog to accompany a human safely on the streets and in public, for which there may well be some device incorporated in it to facilitate tensioning and slackening

DOG-END | dóg-énd |

MEANING: A cigarette butt with enough tobacco left for a person desperate enough to try lighting it up again; a mostly smoked cigarette, picked up from where it was thrown into the gutter

ORIGINS AND HISTORY: An expression now regarded as British slang, although it seems to have been common around the English-speaking world in the 1930s—unless it was a term at that time deliberately (and presumably mistakenly) put in the mouths of American criminals by more than one English crime writer

....

DOGWASH | dóg-wosh |

MEANING: Of minimal urgency; of the lowest priority; virtually optional

ORIGINS AND HISTORY: Said to have originated around 1982 as the last of a list of expressions of urgency with which a certain change in computer software might be necessary—"Wash your dog first"—but probably also relying on the words additionally sounding very close to "hogwash"

The meaning has since been slightly extended to describe something unimportant that is done in order to avoid doing something more important ("displacement activity"). But I ask you: what could possibly be more important than canine cleanliness?

BASSET | bássit |

MEANING: Descriptive of a type of long-eared, short-legged dog once used for hunting foxes and badgers (and therefore also known as a basset hound)

ORIGINS AND HISTORY: "Basset" was not originally the name of a type or breed of dog—it was simply a description, in French, of dogs that were short in stature (*bas*, "low") and relatively small otherwise (*-et*, diminutive suffix); it was first recorded in English in 1616, since when it has apparently always been pronounced in the English fashion, and not the French

Also so called, because it is "lower" than others like it, is the basset horn—a type of orchestral clarinet with a range of notes that goes lower in pitch than ordinary clarinets.

HOUND | hownd|

MEANING: A dog especially suited to hunting because of its speed and stamina when running

ORIGINS AND HISTORY: The word is the standard Germanic term for "dog" (modern German/Danish *Hund*, Norwegian/Swedish *hund*, Dutch *hond*), but since the conquest of England by the Norman French in 1066—for whom dogs were used solely in hunting deer and boar on their aristocratic estates—it has been applied to types of dogs bred specifically for various forms of hunting (including hunting for rabbits, badgers, and smaller animals)

This apparent change of meaning in English is not actually all that remarkable in the light of the fact that the English verb "to hunt" would seem to come from the same Indo-European root, probably originally meaning "to try to catch hold of." Perhaps more surprising is the derivation of the English word hand *(Anglo-Saxon* hond*), again from the same Indo-European root. The hand is thus basically a "grasper." Something that you grasp at in order to understand may be described as a* hint—*which is yet another cognate word, and one that demonstrates how the equally cognate Latin* canis, *"dog," might also suggest that canines in English should be "canny"—able to grasp matters quickly and act accordingly—which is in addition etymologically akin to the verb "to know."*

MASTIFF | mástif |

MEANING: A large type of dog (not originally any specific breed) that looks potentially aggressive, with a large head and drooping ears and a short, thick coat

ORIGINS AND HISTORY: An example of "dog-Latin" (see below) in more than one sense, the word *mastiff* comes from two separate words in Norman French, both deriving from late Latin, one confused with the other. In word shape, the nearer of the two Norman French original words was *mestif*, "mongrel" (originally from Latin *mixtus*, "mixed," modern Spanish *mestizo*); but that word was used in error for Norman French *mastin*, "tamed" (from Latin *mansuetinus*, "habituated over time to manual control," thus "domesticated")—although the implication remained that the domestication might have been difficult and less than perfectly accomplished

....

DOG-LATIN | dóg-láttin |

MEANING: The vocabulary and grammar of Latin spoken and written from the end of the Roman Empire until medieval times (at which point, in theory, Church Latin prevailed); but also the sort of Latin spoken and written by people from that time until today who have not been taught properly or who are not good at it anyway (or who try simply to "latinize" English words)

ORIGINS AND HISTORY: The expression in English was first recorded in 1611 and is one of those in which the word *dog* implies "less than real"

The term was evidently invented by classicists, purists,
and pedants at a time when Latin was beginning to lose
its international currency and educational significance.
It ignores the fact that all languages evolve and change,
and that the Latin of the Roman Republic (510–27
BCE) continually changed and was therefore increasingly
different from the Latin of the Roman Empire (27 BCE–
fifth century CE).

Cave
Canem

DOGFALL | dóg-fawl |

MEANING: A result that is effectively one in which nobody wins; a draw or tie that scores no points or means that everyone has to start over

ORIGINS AND HISTORY: An early nineteenth-century English wrestling term from Cumberland and Westmorland; in that type of wrestling, each of the two contestants holds the other in a bear hug around the waist and tries to twist the other bodily so that he cannot remain standing, and in that way suffers a "fall"; a dogfall occurs when *both* contestants lose their balance and topple over, so that the bout has to begin again

DOGLEG | dóg-leg |

MEANING: A sharp bend joining two straight lengths; a near 90-degree bend in a course or path

ORIGINS AND HISTORY: Derives initially (1703) from the adjective "dog-legged," an architectural term referring to a staircase that had squarish landings and no stairwell or central shaft, and that therefore required people to make a double right-angled turn between flights; more than a century later the description was applied also to a type of golf hole that involved a single sharpish bend in the fairway

Although the present meaning corresponds to an angle of about 90 degrees, the word's derivation makes it clear that the intention was more to suggest a much sharper two-stage turn—like the hind legs of a dog when lying flat.

SNATCH | snach |

MEANING: A quick grab at something or someone, a seizing; a small quantity of a larger whole

ORIGINS AND HISTORY: Like *snack*, originally (1520s) a dialectal variant of *snap*, meaning a "sudden bite" at something (primarily by a dog), thus both a quick grab at something (1550s) and a small amount appropriating to a mouthful (1570s), and thus an excerpt or piece of music or verse (1590s)

Someone who snatches is of course a snatcher. Now a "snatcher" or "body snatcher" was at first (1780s) a term for an officially appointed bailiff who might use forceful methods to apprehend an absconding debtor or felon. But the term took on a far more gruesome meaning in England, where it became the word for a person who dug up freshly buried corpses in church graveyards, to sell them on to professors and doctors for teaching students in anatomical biology classes. It was independently replaced in the United States by "copper" (and later "cop"), after which a "snatcher" became first (1870s) an inefficient pickpocket and then (1890s) a kidnapper.

LASSIE | lássi |

MEANING: A girl, daughter, damsel

ORIGINS AND HISTORY: The dialectal diminutive (*-ie*) of *lass*, the feminine form of the word *lad*, which derives from a personal name in Old Norse, *Ladda*, said however to mean no more or less than "boy," "son" (and likewise equally well attested as *laddie*)

*Given as a name for a (female) dog—especially a border collie trained as a sheepdog—in northern Britain for more than a century, Lassie became a common name for (female) rough collies in the United States after the appearance of the first Lassie movie (*Lassie Come Home*) in 1943. The subsequent movies and TV series thereafter turned the name and character of the dog into something of a cliché, not helped by the slightly more macho nature of Lassie's TV rival, Rin Tin Tin—to the extent that both stars were expected always to be rescuing intemperately foolhardy children from wells by fetching adult assistance.*

MAX | máks |

MEANING: Usually apprehended as an abbreviation of the personal names *Maximilian*, *Maxim*, or *Maxwell*

ORIGINS AND HISTORY: In all of these personal names the first element *max-* ultimately derives from Latin *magnus*, "great," or *maximus*, "greatest"

Apart from the fact that in Latin max- *implied not only "greatest" but "largest," and aside from the fact that in the TV series* Hart to Hart *it was the loyal manservant who was called Max and not the dog, people should perhaps remember that the predominant personage of this name in recent decades was the hero in the eponymous sci-fi action thriller* Mad Max *(1979; sequels so far* The Road Warrior*, 1981, and* Beyond The Thunderdome*, 1985) Nonetheless, Max remains at the top of the list of popular names for a dog in the United States.*

COLLIE, COLLIE DOG | kólli | kólli dog |

MEANING: A type of long-haired sheepdog that was originally bred in Scotland and now known worldwide

ORIGINS AND HISTORY: Although they are generally black and white, it would seem that these sheepdogs are named because of the blackness of the black coloration—it is "coaly," like coal, which when pronounced in the Scottish accent of 1651 evidently sounded like "collie" and was written down in that form at that time

The pronunciation is easier to understand if you recall that coal workers (or coal ships) may alternately be called colliers *and that they work for a* colliery.

POODLE | póod'l |

MEANING: A type of pet dog with long, thick, curly hair that is often clipped short, although sometimes tufts are left long for an effect equating to canine topiary

ORIGINS AND HISTORY: The breed was initially used for hunting near lakes and rivers in Germany, and was therefore called the *Pudelhund* (in which *pudel* is the same as English *puddle*, but actually referred to the dogs' *paddling* or splashing in water [see *dog paddle*, page 110])

The poodle was thus introduced to the English-speaking world as a dog for wealthy landowners on whose estates there were lakes. But it seems that it was their wives who changed first the function and then the character of the dogs. As a pet dog subject to individual coiffure, the poodle became the constant companion of women of high society during the early twentieth century—and impoverished young men who were overly ambitious to follow their example were disdainfully described as "poodle-fakers."

DOGGY EXPRESSIONS & PHRASES

MAN'S BEST FRIEND

MEANING: The dog as loyal companion

ORIGINS AND HISTORY: Attributed (at least in overall sense, if not precisely in those words) to the prominent lawyer and Senator George Graham Vest of Missouri in a (final appeals) court case at the Supreme Court of Missouri in 1870

Senator Vest represented a Mr. Burden, whose dog "Drum" had been shot, apparently accidentally but unapologetically, by a neighbor, Mr. Hornsby. He ended his closing speech with a long and highly emotive paean of praise for canine companions and their good-natured loyalty. His tribute to Man's Best Friend so swayed the jury that it awarded Mr. Burden more than twice the damages for which he was formally suing Mr. Hornsby.

HAIR OF THE DOG

MEANING: An alcoholic drink consumed in order to mitigate the effects of overconsumption the night before; an attempt to relieve or reduce the effects of an activity by partly repeating that activity

ORIGINS AND HISTORY: It was apparently a late medieval folk belief that the pain and infection caused by the bite of a maddened dog could be relieved by applying some of the same dog's hair—possibly in the form of ashes—to the wound; it is very unlikely that anybody actually tried it (or, if they did, that it worked)

The concept of "curing like with like" nonetheless goes back as far as the ancient Greeks, and is—in a very different way—still reckoned to be strangely effective in the practice of alternative medicine known as homeopathy.

PAVLOV'S DOG

MEANING: A person who acts as if psychologically conditioned to react to a stimulus (like the sound of a bell); a person whose responses seem mechanical

ORIGINS AND HISTORY: Russian scientist Ivan Pavlov in the 1880s and 1890s used various stimuli, including a bell, to signal to his dogs that he was about to feed them; in due course he was able to prove that his dogs salivated on presentation of the stimuli even when the food was not forthcoming. He called this a "conditional reflex," which was mistranslated into English as a "conditioned reflex" and became an essential concept in the burgeoning science of psychology

GO TO THE DOGS

MEANING: To be ruined; to get into a bad situation from which recovery is all but impossible

ORIGINS AND HISTORY: From the time of the ancient Greeks and Romans, food deemed no longer fit for human consumption might well "go to the dogs" or be "thrown to the dogs," because the dogs—if they were hungry enough—would ignore the smell and taste and eat it anyway

Yes, amazingly, there was a time when the main source of food for dogs was not a can, a packet, a sachet, a pouch, or a box. Instead, the dogs got scraps from the humans' table—but often only when it was so well and truly disgusting that no human would touch it. It is in this sense that Shakespeare describes some medicine ("physic") that tastes so vile that it is fit only to go "to the dogs"— although even in these modern times medicines are not renowned for their delicious flavors. How very different from the contents of a doggy bag that might be brought home from a top restaurant today . . .

CAVE CANEM

MEANING: Beware of the dog (in Latin)

ORIGINS AND HISTORY: An expression found on the walls and gates of homes in ancient Rome and Pompeii, although the verbal imperative *cave* meant rather more than "beware": it meant "be advised," and was a legal technical term used in contracts and public proclamations

Because of the legal connotations of the verb cavere, *the implication in* cave canem *was that if you were attacked by the dog after having had ample opportunity to read and understand the warning, no legal redress for injury would be available to you. That, after all, is the meaning of the same verb in the expression* caveat emptor, *usually translated as "Let the buyer beware," but in fact implying that no legal redress is available to the buyer once the purchase has been completed, even if the purchased object turns out not to have been what was thought.*

PRAIRIE DOG

MEANING: One of a genus (*Cynomys*) of burrowing rodents—like woodchucks, only smaller—that live in the grasslands of North America

ORIGINS AND HISTORY: The ordinary name for these social animals would seem to be a translation of what they were called by French-speaking explorers in the 1760s, and may in fact correspond to the first usage of the word *prairie* in English—through French, ultimately from late Latin *prataria*, "meadowlike grassy place"

Captain Meriwether Lewis, of the Lewis and Clark Expedition (1804), described prairie dogs as "barking squirrels," and it is because they bark rather like high-pitched dogs, and have a code of barks that evidently provides a system of communication, that they are known as "dogs" at all. The generic name Cynomys *reaffirms the connection, being Latinized Greek for "dog mouse."*

PARIAH DOG

MEANING: A dog that might once have been domesticated, but has since lost its home and turned wild, surviving meagerly on scraps and garbage on the edge of an urban or rural village community, and being chased away on sight by local human residents

ORIGINS AND HISTORY: A term that dates from the period of British colonial and economic domination of much of southern India, and that was first recorded in 1816

The word pariah *is a corruption of the Tamil* paraiyar,
*"drummers"—which perhaps regrettably indicates how
low the status of some hereditary musicians was in Tamil
society at the time, for the term was also the title of one
of the lowest social castes or ranks, whose duties included
providing the player of the large drum beaten at certain
religious festivals. It was, incidentally, from this caste
of people that the British in Madras employed most of
their domestic servants, and it was only after the
word had entered British vocabulary that the
primary meaning "low-caste"
was extended also to the
meaning "outcast(e)."*

MY DOGS ARE BARKING

MEANING: My feet hurt

ORIGINS AND HISTORY: An extension of Victorian London cockney rhyming slang; in the 1890s, "dogs" was an abbreviation of "dogs' meat," rhyming slang for "feet" (first recorded with that meaning in the United States in 1913); "barking" because that is what dogs do when they are persistently annoying

Since the 1920s, the cockney rhyming slang for "feet" has instead been "plates," short for "plates of meat." It may have been shortages of meat during World War I (1914–1918) that were responsible for such an evident rise in meat's status, from being set out for dogs through being put on plates.

LOVE ME, LOVE MY DOG

MEANING: If you love me, a mere human, you must also worship and adore my canine companion, next to whom I am but a shadow; if you love me, you will have to accept all the baggage that comes with me

ORIGINS AND HISTORY: The second of those meanings was what Saint Bernard of Clairvaux was getting at when he wrote the expression (in Latin) in around 1150, partly with reference to the love of God and the need to fulfill all the requirements of a disciplined Christian life in order to be sure of experiencing it

In the light of that moral severity, it will come as no surprise to note that Saint Bernard of Clairvaux was not the Saint Bernard for whom the Saint Bernard dogs were named (or, indeed, the Saint Bernard Pass in the Swiss Alps, where those dogs were first trained to rescue travelers in winter emergencies). That was Saint Bernard of Menthon—alternately described as Bernard of Montjoux and Archdeacon Bernard of Aosta—who died about a decade before Saint Bernard of Clairvaux was born.

CANINE TEETH

MEANING: The sharp-pointed teeth at the front corners of the mouth of almost all mammals and some reptiles, technically called cuspids; known in cats, dogs, and reptiles as fangs, and in the human upper jaw as eye teeth

ORIGINS AND HISTORY: Evidently it was dogs (especially wolves) that seemed to humans to be the classic animal with such teeth, for they have been described as "dog's" teeth for well over two millennia—just as the word *dogtooth* describes the sharp-pointed shape of a canine tooth of any species

Historic as the association of such teeth with dogs is, it should be noted that in terms of paleontology, "canine" teeth appeared well before canine animals—and actually before the (true) dinosaurs. In modern animals the tusks of wild boars and walruses are modified canines, but the tusks of elephants are in fact modified incisors.

HIS BARK IS WORSE THAN HIS BITE

MEANING: What he threatens to do, and how he threatens to do it, is generally much more violent than what he actually does

ORIGINS AND HISTORY: This would seem to be a relatively modern extension of an originally sixteenth-century English proverb, "Barking dogs seldom bite"; the modern expression suggests that the recipient of the threat should at least experience both bark and bite and therefore be in a position to make a decisive judgment on which is worse, whereas the older expression expects the recipient to be able to escape with just the bark, however ferocious

Strangely, it is the sixteenth-century version that other European languages tend to fondly believe is their own. In French dictionaries, for example, un chien qui aboie ne mord pas *("a dog that barks does not bite") is always given as the translation of "his bark is worse than his bite"; the Italian is identical (but in Italian), as is the German (in German). Ah—you'll be wanting the Basque version. OK, here it is:* txakurzaunkaria ez da horzkaria.

WORK LIKE A DOG

MEANING: To work flat out; to put all your effort into your work

ORIGINS AND HISTORY: Regrettably, there have been times in history when humans have taken advantage of the pack instincts of dogs to work them so hard in teams that some of them die; it has long been an established fact, therefore, that dogs can (relatively willingly) work themselves to death—although such a sense is rarely intended in the modern usage of this now entirely figurative expression

It is by working like a dog that you become "dog tired"—in which case you may crash out on the nearest available floor space, all limbs splayed, snoring stertorously as family members carefully step over and around you.

GO AND SEE A MAN ABOUT A DOG

MEANING: To go away and do other things you have to do; to disappear from view for a period of time

ORIGINS AND HISTORY: An expression that was coined by Dion Boucicault in his play *The Flying Scud* (1866)—a horseracing melodrama alternatively titled *A Four-Legged Fortune*—in order to get an unwanted character (an old and crotchety jockey) off stage

Boucicault (born Dionysius Lardner Boursiquot—his father was a French refugee in Ireland) was educated in London, England, became a successful though controversial playwright, moved to the United States in 1853, but returned to England seven years later. Alltogether he wrote more than 200 plays, in most of which he also starred on stage, specializing in roles that required a broad Irish accent. Whereas The Flying Scud *is now virtually unknown and unplayable, this expression—a feeble excuse to escape from a potentially awkward situation—has remained a cliché ever since.*

ONCE BITTEN, TWICE SHY

MEANING: An event that produces a bad experience is sensibly avoided thereafter

ORIGINS AND HISTORY: Various expressions with much the same meaning have appeared in English since before the time of Chaucer—such as "A burnt child dreads the fire" (1320)—and William Caxton's translation of Aesop's fables (1484) contains at least two stories with the same moral; however, it was not until the 1850s that the notion of biting arose in this context, and only in the 1890s that the exact wording of the phrase was first recorded, in *Folk Phrases of Four Counties* by G. F. Northall

DOGGONE, DOGGONE IT

MEANING: Damn, dammit

ORIGINS AND HISTORY: A careful and deliberate distortion of "God damn!" and "God dammit!" first printed in 1851, although a slightly earlier version of the longer expression was "dog on it" (as if somehow parallel with, for example, "plague on it!")

This expression was coined as a polite, but entirely comprehensible alternative to an imprecation that was too shocking for nice people to say or write . . . although not-so-nice people were saying and writing it—to such an extent that it has by now lost most of its force.

RUN AWAY WITH HIS TAIL BETWEEN HIS LEGS

MEANING: To flee in abject humiliation; to rapidly withdraw in total defeat and shame

ORIGINS AND HISTORY: The expression is a direct description of how a dog defeated in a dogfight runs away, and as such, is as old as the language

Until the moment of defeat, the tail remains outstanding and is part of the dog's challenge to its opponent (a dogfight often involves considerable tail-chasing [see dogfight, *page 14]). On accepting defeat, however, the dog not only signifies the fact by removing the challenge, but also prudently makes as swiftly as possible to remove the rest of his body from the threat of hostile dental treatment. This mode of rapid withdrawal is evidently the opposite of "hightailing" it (as some monkeys do). One more thing: whereas in former centuries it might have been a relatively common event, it is extremely rare these days for anyone to witness a dogfight; dogs tend to live so well that there is little need to fight others or even to show aggression— except of course for essential demonstrations of macho toughness to impress other dogs.*

PUTTING ON THE DOG

MEANING: Acting or dressing in an ostentatiously smooth way

ORIGINS AND HISTORY: An expression first recorded in 1871, apparently extending the contemporaneous usage of "dog" as an adjective meaning "flashy," "showy"; until at least the 1940s the expression was "to put on dog"—with no "the"

The notion of smartness and suavity was further extended at the end of the twentieth century when in certain circles the word "dog" came to be used as a term of address (such as "pal") for male persons of only fleeting acquaintance.

DONE/DRESSED UP LIKE A DOG'S DINNER

MEANING: Early twentieth-century British slang for "looking uncharacteristically smart," "looking suspiciously neatly prepared"

ORIGINS AND HISTORY: This would seem to be a jokey reference to how dog food was improving as social conditions also got better—so much so that dogs might be expected to have a formal meal like "dinner"

On the other hand, to look "like a dog's breakfast" was, in the same slang context, to appear to have been dragged backward through a rain-soaked hedge several times.

CANARY ISLANDS

MEANING: English name of a group of volcanic islands some 60 miles (100 kilometers) west of the mainland coast of southern Morocco, in northwest Africa

ORIGINS AND HISTORY: Roman geographers first heard of the islands from the geographical accounts of them by one Juba, ruler of a north African kingdom, in the first century BCE; it was from Juba's description of them as overrun by wild dogs that the Roman author Pliny called the islands *Canaria* ("place of dogs," from *canes*, "dogs")

For many centuries the islands were the furthest westerly point of the known world for Europeans. It was the islands that gave their name to the birds now called canaries in English (originally "Canary birds," in the same way that wine from the islands was called "Canary wine").

IN THE DOGHOUSE

MEANING: In disgrace

ORIGINS AND HISTORY: Mid-twentieth-century U.S. humorous slang, featured in many newspaper and movie cartoons involving a rueful husband obliged to tell the household pet to move over to make room for him in the dog's accommodation

Because of its supposed small size and distinct lack of home comforts, "the doghouse" has meant various things in U.S. slang since the 1920s. To some criminals and to the police it once meant a spare garage in a residential area, hired by vehicle thieves to store a stolen vehicle until the heat was off and the vehicle could be moved on to another area or to the chop shop. To other criminals it meant a watchtower on the top of a prison wall. And to a railroad hobo it meant a trackside calaboose or jail.

LET SLEEPING DOGS LIE

MEANING: To leave things as they are, even though they are not entirely satisfactory (the implication being that to take any action might stir up real trouble, with grave consequences for all concerned)

ORIGINS AND HISTORY: Apparently an English proverb dating from as long ago as the fourteenth century

Many dog-owning authors have commented on the fact that sleeping dogs don't just lie—the deeper they sleep, the heavier they weigh on top of the bed (and on the humans in it), the louder their snores and snuffles reverberate, and the more violent their dream reactions become. Whether to let a sleeping dog lie can, in such circumstances, turn into a Serious Moral Issue.

MUD PUPPY

MEANING: A large aquatic salamander of the northern and eastern United States

ORIGINS AND HISTORY: First recorded as such in 1859—though it must surely have been called that (or something else) before then

Also described as a "water dog" from the same date, the mud puppy is found mainly from the Great Lakes in the north down to Georgia in the south. Elsewhere in the United States the term may be applied instead to any of several other kinds of salamander, notably the hellbender. In some areas the mud puppy is alternately known as the dogfish, although a dogfish is more commonly a name for smaller types of shark [see dogfish, page 49].

THE DOG AND DUCK

MEANING: A once-popular name for pubs in England

ORIGINS AND HISTORY: Another hunting reference: owners of estates would use one to hunt the other [see also *bird-dog*, page 53]—and might return with both to the local alehouse on the way back home

SLUSH PUPPY

MEANING: A strongly flavored drink containing finely crushed ("shaved") ice

ORIGINS AND HISTORY: Before "slush puppies" became a term for a huge selection of alcoholic cocktails served with shaved ice, they were drinks for kids featuring sugary fruit cordials and ice crystals small enough to get through a fairly hefty straw; the name probably therefore derives from the notion that a kid who plays in mud is a "mud puppy," and a kid who enjoys slush (partly melted snow during a thaw) is thus a "slush puppy." Regrettably—but entirely understandably, if the intention is to avoid the connotations of an alcoholic content—the name has in recent years been hijacked by a proprietary manufacturer of children's drinks, who seems to believe that the singular of "slush puppies" is "slush puppie"

Puppies and other dogs have long been associated, one way or another, with drinks—alcoholic or otherwise [see hair of the dog, page 71]. Perhaps the most far-flung expressions in that regard have been a couple that were transported from nineteenth-century London all the way south to Australia, where they remained current for decades longer. Completely comprehensible at sight is "dog's soup," meaning "water." Rather more obscure is "dog's nose," which apparently meant (and in some bars still means) a mixture of gin and beer, involving twelve parts of beer to one of gin. Perhaps you have to say "Muzzle-tov" before you drink it.

BE SOLD A PUP

MEANING: Acquire or receive something that is not at all what it was purported to be; get something that is far less than expected and/or paid for

ORIGINS AND HISTORY: Criminal slang of the early the twentieth century—and as such, originally expressing the same event from the opposite viewpoint: "to sell someone a pup" meant to swindle a dupe or pull off a scam

The basic notion is evidently that the dupe, gull, patsy, or john is landed with a "pup" in place of the full-grown dog that he or she had reckoned proudly to possess. Yet today, for many families, having a pup in the house is as enjoyable and as valued as having the time-, space-, and food-consuming adult.

THAT DOG WON'T HUNT

MEANING: That option won't work, that idea is a no-no

ORIGINS AND HISTORY: Around 1933 in the southern United States, hunters had so low an opinion of dogs that were untrained, or too old or too stupid to hunt, that they were regarded as worse than useless

The expression effectively means "You're wasting your time, buddy. You won't get anywhere with that. Don't say I didn't warn you." But it's a lot shorter.

WHY KEEP A DOG AND BARK YOURSELF?

MEANING: There is no point in insisting on doing yourself what you have in fact paid others to do for you

ORIGINS AND HISTORY: A "saying" that was first recorded—in the form "Do not keep a dog and bark yourself"—in sixteenth-century England

A dog that you keep and that barks on your behalf is a form of guard dog (preferably a Rottweiler–alligator crossbreed). This expression is commonly said to have originated at a time when wealthy middle-class social climbers were finding it embarrassingly difficult to delegate household tasks to their new servants—but the original circumstances must in fact have been far more confrontational.

DOG DAYS

MEANING: The hottest days of summer; days when it is so hot that it is almost impossible to do anything but lie around panting with your tongue out

ORIGINS AND HISTORY: An ancient Roman expression—but based on astronomical lore from much earlier still—relating the hottest days of summer to the nights on which the Dog Star, Sirius, appears above the horizon, rises to a zenith, and descends again; by Roman tradition, this lasted fifty days (but of course it depended on the observer's latitude, and has changed slightly over the millennia)

Sirius, the brightest star in the night sky, was called the Dog Star because it dominates the constellation of Canis Major (the Great Dog [see cynosure, page 29]). Because it was so conspicuous, and because it did not appear all the year around, it was the major chronological reference for periods of time longer than days (measured by the sun) and months (measured by the moon) for ancient Babylonian astronomers. Through studying Sirius (which they called Set), the ancient Egyptians were aware that the solar year is 365¼ days long. Meanwhile, the ancient Greeks knew Sirius as Kuōn Seirios, the "Ultra-Hot Dog."

DOG IN THE MANGER

MEANING: A person unwilling to let other people have or do something, even though their having it or doing it is of no actual consequence or value to the first person

ORIGINS AND HISTORY: Derives from a fable of Aesop (sixth century BCE, although he amounts pretty much to a fable himself) about a dog who positioned himself on top of a manger—a hay trough—inside a farmyard barn and would not allow the farm's ox or horse near the manger to eat the hay in it, although he had no desire to eat the hay himself

It has been suggested (but so far only by Professor Marvin) that this expression is an unfortunate corruption of "dog is the manager," and that Aesop's fable was originally meant to show the natural primacy of the canine species over all other mammals for their mutual benefit.

CHERRY HOG

MEANING: Dog (in the cockney rhyming slang of nineteenth-century London)

ORIGINS AND HISTORY: Many commentators today believe that the "hog" of a cherry was the stone or pit, and that quite incidentally there was at the same time a popular children's game called cherry hog, which involved throwing cherry stones into a small hole excavated for the purpose; however, research reveals that the cherry stone has never been called a "hog," but that "hog" could mean "pit"—the kind of pit that was the hole into which the children threw the cherry stones

In other words, the derivation of the expression was the name of the game, but the game was so called for its target and not for the missile propelled toward the target. The game must have been amazingly popular for its name to have become part of the folk-cultural language of Victorian London. And it does suggest that at least the kids were getting some fruit to eat.

DOG AND BONE

MEANING: "Phone" in modern London cockney rhyming slang

ORIGINS AND HISTORY: It would be nice to suggest that this is one of the really early expressions of cockney rhyming slang, dating from the early 1800s—but telephones were not in popular use much before the early 1900s, and not in widespread general public use in England until perhaps the 1930s; this expression first became popular in London during the 1960s

Like most dogs, Professor Marvin is an enthusiastic osteophage—although he is appalled that many of the bone-shaped items given to him to eat, bite, or otherwise play with are not bones at all. Some are made of hardish biscuit, others of pathetically soft cake. Some are even of rubber and are intended to exercise his jaw muscles. But all are of the classic bone shape. And that is very interesting, etymologically—because the classic bone shape to us is that of the largest and boniest bone of the human *body: the femur, which runs from hip to knee. It is the essential leg bone. And that is why in English the word* bone *is cognate with the word that in most other Germanic languages means "leg"* (German Bein, *Dutch* been, *Norwegian/Swedish/Danish* ben).

SICK AS A DOG

MEANING: Very sick, barfing all over the place, prostrate with nausea, suffering from polyemesis

ORIGINS AND HISTORY: An expression first mentioned in print in English in 1705, although no one knows the real reason why it should be dogs that are so sick . . . except that dogs are, regrettably, associated with vomiting in the Bible ("the dog returns to its vomit"—Proverbs 26:11)

In the United States this expression has been static as it is for more than 100 years. In Britain, however, it has since 1979 been overtaken by the expression "sick as a parrot"—which is surprising for several reasons, most notably that birds are not and cannot be sick to the degree of vomiting (although some may deliberately regurgitate food for their young).

BLACK DOG

MEANING: Lingering clinical depression; persistent grumpiness, apparently willful irascibility

ORIGINS AND HISTORY: First recorded in the most serious sense in 1826, the expression is now often associated with the writings of Winston Churchill, whose prolonged bouts of potentially suicidal depression he himself called his "black dog"

Some highly commendable national organizations founded to help people deal with deep depression (and which therefore, to some extent, overlap with the functions of the Samaritans) work under the name Black Dog, notably in the Republic of Ireland and in Australia. Strangely, however, there is no real explanation for the term—is the "black dog" meant to follow closely behind, to loom over, or even to ride on the back of the sufferer? No one knows.

DOG TAG

MEANING: A small metal plate with details of identification stamped onto it, made to hang on a collar, neckchain, or wristband

ORIGINS AND HISTORY: In the United States, dog tags were first meant to identify and return dogs that got lost from their homes. From the time of the American Civil War (the 1860s), however, the term applied also to identification tags for military personnel in the field of combat, primarily intended to identify the dead in battle or to give personal medical information about a soldier wounded and unable to talk. Note, incidentally, that the slang term for an ordinary infantryman is "dogface"

From the mid-1990s, the term "dog tag" has been unofficially dropped in favor of the more technical "ID tag." At the same time, the fashion has grown for civilians to wear as jewelry similar tags (still called "dog tags") featuring less formal, more individual personal details.

DOG BISCUIT

MEANING: A hard, dry cracker for dogs, made of reshaped ground food; slang for "hardtack," also known as ship biscuit, sea bread, or pilot biscuit—a compacted nutritious biscuit designed to resist spoiling and remain edible during sea voyages

ORIGINS AND HISTORY: The slang term dates from U.S. Navy usage around the 1940s; otherwise, the word *biscuit* is directly from French *bis-cuit*, "twice cooked"— heated once to bake it, and heated again to harden it

SEA DOG

MEANING: An old sailor, otherwise known as an "old salt"; a privateer or pirate, also known as a "sea rover"; or a common or harbor seal (*Calocephalus vitulinus*)

ORIGINS AND HISTORY: In fact, today's primary meaning—an old sailor—is the most recent, recorded first in 1840 and popularized thereafter in works by authors such as Robert Louis Stevenson and Rafael Sabatini; the earliest use of the expression was in relation to the common seal (1598), and even then may correspond to no more than a translation from contemporary German or Dutch—or from an even earlier equivalent expression in Goidelic (Scottish and Irish) Gaelic, actually referring to the sea otter (*Lutra* species)

TO LIE DOGGO

MEANING: To lie low and keep a low profile, to keep quiet and out of the way, to stay hidden but keep watch

ORIGINS AND HISTORY: Apparently first evidenced in print in 1893, and coined directly as a reference to the way dogs were then thought to behave in situations where discretion was the better part of valor

A major U.S. dictionary of American slang suggests that the expression derives from "a trained dog's playing dead." Most commentators scoff at this, declaring that dogs need no such training in the art. But in this case both dictionary and commentators have lost sight of the actual meaning. It is not "to play dead" but "to actively keep a low profile," "to be careful to not be seen."

TO DOG IT

MEANING: To chicken out, to evade (something), to avoid doing (something), to run away from (something)

ORIGINS AND HISTORY: Originally U.S. criminal slang of the late 1920s, probably derived from the expression "to run away [like a dog] with his tail between his legs," but quickly thereafter taken into general usage—especially by kids who reckoned to "dog school"

Some commentators have suggested that in this expression the word dog *might be a variant of "dodge." Kids can, after all, dodge school. Unhappily for those commentators,* dodge *is indeed a variant of another word—but that word is not* dog, *it is* duck. *You duck out of something by keeping your head down, diving beneath the surface, and so avoiding it. The birds we call "ducks" are so described because they too can dive beneath the surface to avoid the hunter with his gun. And of course, in the same way, kids can duck school. All this leaves us with a linguistic anomaly. I can "man" a post or station in some formal grouping or organized arrangement—but Professor Marvin cannot "dog" it and still be present.*

DOG ZEBRA

MEANING: U.S. Navy term for a state of readiness on board in anticipation of bad weather or a requirement for total lights blackout, effectively "securing all openings" so that they are airtight, watertight, firetight, and fumetight

ORIGINS AND HISTORY: This is actually an extension to the naval term Condition Zebra (as opposed to Condition X-ray or Condition Yoke) for which relevant fittings (doors, hatches, and other means of access) are clearly marked

Essentially, the term represents just the letters D and Z as used to code a ship's fittings—but the names for the letters derive from the old Morse code telegraphy letters (in which A, B, C, and D were Able, Baker, Charlie, and Dog) popularly used in World War II, and not the more recent radio code words for letters as used by police forces (in which A, B, C, and D are Alpha, Bravo, Charlie, and Delta).

DOG WATCH(ES)

MEANING: In the navy, the two two-hour spells of duty ("on watch") between 4 and 8 p.m.

ORIGINS AND HISTORY: For officers and sailors in the (British) Royal Navy at the beginning of the 1700s, the twenty-four hours of the day were divided into five four-hour watches and two two-hour watches; the two-hour watches were between four and six in the afternoon and between six and eight in the evening; those not on duty for one of those two-hour durations could snatch a bit of shut-eye, in what we might now call a "cat nap," but what in those days was instead known as a "dog sleep"; those who were required to stay awake while others got their dog sleep were therefore on dog watch

The shorter dog watches not only ensured that navy men varied their spells on and off duty on a forty-eight-hour basis, but allowed for the two sittings of the rudimentary supper for the whole ship's company each side of the six o' clock ("four bells") deadline between the watches.

LET DOG SEE RABBIT

MEANING: Get out of the way and let me see what's going on; you are obscuring my view—MOVE!

ORIGINS AND HISTORY: An expression evidently taken from rabbit coursing (the organized hunting of rabbits enclosed within the grounds of a country house or manor) in northern England, probably during the second half of the nineteenth century. A rabbit would be "sprung" by a gamekeeper or his dog and would run out into the open; the hunter would hold his hound until he was sure that the dog had seen the rabbit, and then let the dog go; it was then judged on how fast it caught and dispatched the rabbit. For the purposes of accurate judging, therefore, it was important to ensure that the dog had seen the rabbit before being let loose

Whether genuinely or facetiously, the expression would seem to come from the north of England (especially Yorkshire), where people wouldn't normally say "Let the dog see the rabbit."

....

A DOG'S LIFE

MEANING: A life hardly worth living; a life of subservience, drudgery, and misery

ORIGINS AND HISTORY: An expression first recorded in the sixteenth century, which then gained in popularity until the end of the nineteenth century, but which had already begun to be taken less seriously by 1918, when Charlie Chaplin made a shortish (forty-minute) silent movie of the same name featuring The Little Tramp and his faithful pooch in a struggle to survive in the inner city

Charlie Chaplin not only starred in the movie A Dog's Life, but also wrote the book for it, and produced and directed it. His brother Sydney Chaplin also played a bit part in it, but, according to most commentators, was far outperformed by the dog, Scraps. Some ninety years later, ever-changing social conditions have meant that for a growing majority of people the expression "a dog's life" suggests a pleasantly cushy existence.

HOT DOG

MEANING: A hot frankfurter/wiener (with or without mustard, onions, and other ingredients) in a roll

ORIGINS AND HISTORY: First mentioned in print in the *Yale Record* of October 1895, although "dogs" had by then been a term for wieners for around fifty years—since the makers of sausages were first accused of economizing by using dog meat

Also in the 1890s, a "hot dog" was an expression used for a particularly smartly dressed college student. Within a further twenty years the same expression implied not only smartness in dress, but also special facility in professional or sporting activity. Today, it is used mostly in association with extreme (i.e. risky, dangerous) sports and other hazardous ventures. In parallel, "Hot dog!" has been used as an expression of surprise for almost as long, although it began as a means of avoiding using the potentially offensive phrase "My God!" or "Good God!" It has the emphatic form "Hot diggity (or diggety) dog!", which was used, for example, as the major part of the title of a popular song (to a theme from Rhapsody: España *by Emmanuel Chabrier) in 1956, sung by Perry Como and others. Great-grandpa might just remember it.*

DOG'S EYE AND DEAD 'ORSE

MEANING: Meat pie and tomato sauce (in Australia)

ORIGINS AND HISTORY: Mid-twentieth-century Australian rhyming slang

Note that this expression could only have become popular once the term "dog's eye" was known independently well enough to be used subsequently to mean something else. From the 1920s (until at least the 1960s) to "give someone the dog's eye" was to either stare directly at a person or to give a cool sidelong glance at them. I must admit that when Professor Marvin feels obliged to look reproachfully long and hard at me—generally when I've committed some quite unspeakable solecism such as inadvertently putting a finger in his water bowl—I really do feel a bit like a dead 'orse.

HAVEN'T SEEN YOU IN A DOG'S AGE

MEANING: Haven't seen you for a very long while

ORIGINS AND HISTORY: An informal twentieth-century American expression that is now slightly outmoded

The inclusion of the word "dog's" in this expression would appear to be more for emphasis than for any specific meaning. After all, a dog's age, by common calculation, would be seven times shorter in years than a human age—since one human year is reckoned to correspond to seven canine years. On the other hand, perhaps "a dog's age" is a corrupt adaptation of the British slang phrase "donkey's years," originally (in 1916) "donkey's ears," implying "extra-long."

TWO DOGS STRIVE FOR A BONE, AND A THIRD RUNS AWAY WITH IT

MEANING: The only one who benefits from an argument between two parties may be a third party altogether

ORIGINS AND HISTORY: Recorded as a "saying" (that is, a proverb) in the 1570s

It is hard to believe this was ever a much-used expression, since it seems to tell a story more than it makes a point.

THE TAIL WAGGING THE DOG

MEANING: A minority or lesser part controlling the majority or greater part

ORIGINS AND HISTORY: An expression first recorded in 1907 and not thereafter well evidenced until the 1960s

Because of the association with minorities and majorities, this expression is often used in the context of political commentary, especially when the "minorities" and "majorities" involved are those of an unpreferred political persuasion and the phrase can be used as a sneer at both factions.

DOG PADDLE

MEANING: In swimming, an informal kind of stroke involving the churning of the arms and legs without bringing them out of the water, the result being a slow and somewhat tiring movement forward

ORIGINS AND HISTORY: Evidently named for the way dogs swim, although the verb *paddle* (like *puddle*) in the early sixteenth century meant—and still today properly means—only "to splash around at the water's edge" [see *poodle*, page 66]

....

RAINING CATS AND DOGS

MEANING: Raining very heavily indeed

ORIGINS AND HISTORY: Apparently dating from a sixteenth-century analogy (recorded in 1579) to the noise and ferocity of a fight between a dog and a cat; variants of the expression became common in the early 1650s (Henry Vaughn: "Dogs and Cats rained in showre," *Olor Iscanus*, 1651; Richard Brome: "It shall raine . . . Dogs and Polecats," *The City Wit*, 1653; although it was not until 1738 that it appeared as above in *Polite Conversations*, a satirical work on the subject of clichés by Jonathan Swift

Those who suggest that the expression derives from heavy rain's flooding out dead cats and dogs from overwhelmed eighteenth-century urban drains forget that other, lighter, but equally malodorous dead animals would be washed out first and in greater (more memorable) numbers.

TOY DOG

MEANING: A class of dogs defined differently by different canine authorities, but chiefly comprising small dogs that in general are considered pet (or companion) dogs rather than working dogs; some individual breeds (like the poodle) thus have toy varieties in addition to standard or larger varieties

ORIGINS AND HISTORY: The application of the description "toy" to dogs dates from 1877, although the word itself, meaning "plaything," derives probably from late medieval Dutch toward the end of the sixteenth century

Dogs that are even smaller than toy dogs have in recent years come to be described as "tiny dogs" or even "teacup dogs," although kennel clubs do not use—and may even severely frown upon the use of—such terms.

EVERY DOG HAS ITS DAY

MEANING: To every person—no matter how humble, poor, or young, and no matter how long the wait for it is—will come a moment of triumph, of recognition, of effort rewarded, when he or she is the right person in the right place at the right time

ORIGINS AND HISTORY: An expression dating from the time of King Henry VIII of England (reigned 1509–1547), but apparently nothing to do with his desperate search for the next of his many wives; in fact, it was first printed in one of several books of *Proverbs* by John Heywood in 1546

Henry's daughter Elizabeth, eight years before she became Queen Elizabeth I, is quoted as saying, "Notwithstanding, as a dog hath a day, so may I perchance have time to declare it in deeds," which was either perspicacious of her or good rewriting of history afterward by her press agent. A few decades later, Shakespeare in Hamlet *was displaying his street cred with royalty by declaring, "dog will have his day . . ." (Act 5, scene 1, line 285). Professor Marvin is still waiting in eager anticipation.*

DOG EAT DOG

MEANING: Characterized by unprecedentedly vicious and ruthless infighting

ORIGINS AND HISTORY: Dates from 1931 (in the expression "it's a dog-eat-dog world"), apparently as an extension of a much older "proverb"—"*dog does not eat dog*"—listed in the *Oxford English Dictionary* as dating from "before 1858"; the older expression points out that in general dogs may fight, but they do not eat each other—to which the modern expression rejoins that for them, in that case, to get out the knives and forks makes for a truly scary scenario

When dogs fight, there is usually a clear winner and a clear loser, and the loser runs or slinks off to lick his wounds—because dogs' saliva contains healing enzymes (unlike human saliva).

MAN BITES DOG

MEANING: Sensational news, embodying the implication that people are more affected by an unusual event—especially by the reverse of the usual—than they are by a repetition of the usual

ORIGINS AND HISTORY: Comes from a definition of "news" in the *New York Sun* in 1882 by Charles Anderson Dana: "When a dog bites a man that is not news—but when a man bites a dog, that *is* news."

....

BARING ONE'S TEETH

MEANING: Retracting one's lips to snarl (like a dog), grimacing in a threatening manner, visibly preparing to attack

ORIGINS AND HISTORY: A description of snarling that contains no reference to sound and that uses language as old as Middle English (from around 1320)

All the same, other modern uses of the verb "to bare" in relation to the human frame tend to be rather literary (bare one's head, bare one's bosom) or rather metaphysical (bare one's feelings, bare one's soul). I guess that if I got so old as to have only one tooth left and nonetheless wished to put on a show of ferocity, I would have to grin and bare it.

DOG'S LETTER

MEANING: The letter (and the phonetic pronunciation of) "r"

ORIGINS AND HISTORY: The letter r was most famously described by playwright Ben Jonson in 1636 as the dog's letter because a long, rolled r sounds like a dog's growl; but even then he was in fact quoting the tendentiously obscure Latin author Persius (Aulus Persius Flaccus, 34–62 CE), who called the letter *canina littera* (*Satires*, I, 109) for the same reason

In a scene (Act 2, scene 4) in Romeo and Juliet *that contains some of the most cleverly disguised sexually explicit slang expressions in contemporary English, Shakespeare—writing some forty years before Ben Jonson—also demonstrated that he knew about the letter's description as the "dog's letter." Only because Juliet's nurse—who makes the reference—has been shown earlier in the scene to be both illiterate and scatty, she suggests that the letter r is not the "dog's letter," but the actual name of a dog.*

DOG THROW

MEANING: The lowest throw at dice, especially when two or more dice are being used

ORIGINS AND HISTORY: Another expression taken in translation directly from Latin *canis* (which had in fact borrowed it in translation from ancient Greek *kuōn*)

With this meaning, the expression is now uncommon in English. In fact, if you search for "dog throw" on the Internet, almost all the responses will be about smallish decorated blankets for dogs—a meaning for the expression so new and so American that it has yet to reach some reputable British and Australian-English dictionaries.

LET SLIP THE DOGS OF WAR

MEANING: Let violence reign, let bloody deeds be done, let all hell break loose

ORIGINS AND HISTORY: Part of the soliloquy by Mark Antony vowing to avenge his friend and leader Julius Caesar's murder by the plotters in the Senate on the Ides of March, as written by Shakespeare (*Julius Caesar*, Act 3, scene 1)

The quotation begins "Cry Havoc! and let slip . . ." Now the term "Havoc!" in the fourteenth and fifteenth centuries was a military command, at which the foot soldiers understood they were to break ranks and fall upon an already retreating enemy in an orgy of murder and destruction, leaving none alive and killing any of the enemy's camp followers or servants they could find. It was effectively a command to commit war crimes— and it turned men who perpetrated such atrocities from humans into the "dogs of war"—otherwise exemplified by the ferocious dogs used as personal bodyguards in battle by the leading aristocratic knights.

DOG SOLDIER

MEANING: A member of a warrior faction of the Cheyenne tribe famous for its resistance to U.S. territorial dominance during the 1860s

ORIGINS AND HISTORY: The foremost warrior society of the Cheyenne tribe called themselves Dog Soldiers or Dog Men (in the Cheyenne language), for a tribal legend about dogs who turned into human warriors in order to defend their kin

Membership of the Dog Soldiers—one of five Cheyenne warrior societies, each with its own traditions—guaranteed a particularly honored status among Cheyenne tribespeople, but required an obligation in defensive combat to refuse to retreat, even when not to retreat meant certain death. And this was at a time when fierce and bloody battle was a relatively frequent experience, partly because the comparatively recent acquisition of horses enabled what had been an essentially nomadic farming people to travel further and faster into new territories—until U.S. troops began to try to confine the Cheyenne to a reservation. Resistance (naturally perceived as defense of the tribe) was thenceforward a special responsibility of the Dog Soldiers.

TO BARK AT THE MOON

MEANING: To react violently or noisily but to no purpose whatsoever; to clamor for something knowing perfectly well that you won't get it

ORIGINS AND HISTORY: Originally "to bark against the moon" in medieval English

In Shakespeare's time the expression was alternately "to bay the moon": Brutus, in Julius Caesar *(Act 4, scene 3), says, "I would rather be a dog, and bay the moon, than such a Roman . . ." Hounds, in particular, are still said to bay, rather than bark, when hunting. And a hunted animal when finally cornered is said to turn "at bay"—that is, toward the barking of the dogs, while making whatever noise it can for itself.*

BARKING UP THE WRONG TREE

MEANING: Completely missing the point, working on a false assumption, aiming at the wrong target

ORIGINS AND HISTORY: An expression drawn from life, first printed in *Legends of the West* by James Hall in 1833, thereafter seized on and used figuratively by U.S. journalists from coast to coast

A dog that has chased a squirrel or a raccoon up a tree may not notice if the animal manages to leap over to another nearby tree, and may remain barking at the foot of what is then the wrong tree, much to the exasperation of any accompanying human.

BARKING MAD

MEANING: Loony, barmy, completely crazy (mainly in British and Australian slang)

ORIGINS AND HISTORY: Derived specifically from the connection between barking and the moon—because the moon is responsible for lunacy (Latin *luna*, "the moon") and for lunatics, who are for that reason "loony"

IF YOU LIE DOWN WITH DOGS, YOU GET UP WITH FLEAS

MEANING: If you hang out with a bad crowd, you will end up with the same bad reputation—the classic form of guilt by association

ORIGINS AND HISTORY: Not known, although the two main suggestions are: 1) that it derives from Ireland or northern England at the end of the nineteenth century; 2) that it was an expression used by film actress Jean Harlow (1911–1937)

In the United States an additional meaning for the expression since the 1930s has been that if you sleep around, you might expect to experience unpleasant physical consequences. From the 1980s, however, critics have also particularly associated the expression with political comment on national foreign policy.

....

YOU CAN'T TEACH AN OLD DOG NEW TRICKS

MEANING: A person who has been accustomed for a long time to doing things in one way cannot suddenly change and do things differently, even if it is conspicuously quicker or easier

ORIGINS AND HISTORY: A "proverb" dating from the sixteenth century

Modern psychologists say that, as it stands, it isn't true: both staid old humans and grizzly old dogs can learn new things, and—depending on innate ability or learned facility—can do so quickly and easily. Perhaps this is why the original expression is just as likely to have been "It is hard to teach an old dog new tricks," in which the emphasis is as much on teaching as on learning. Either way, the real answer may be to acquire a new dog. But don't tell Professor Marvin.

INDEX

L
Lassie 64
Latin 20–21, 37, 38, 47,
    60–61, 65, 73, 74,
    116, 117
lead, dog lead 32
let dog see rabbit 104
let sleeping dogs lie 87
let slip the dogs of
    war 118
lie doggo 100
lie down with dogs, get
    up with fleas 122
Lincoln, Abraham 20
litter 13
love me, love my dog
    76–77
lupus 47
lurcher 42
lycanthropy 47

M
man bites dog 115
man's best friend 70
Marvin, Professor 7, 10,
    16, 41, 93, 95, 101,
    107, 113, 123
mastiff 60
Max 65
mongrel 26
mud puppy 88
mutt 11
muzzle 30

N
Normans, Norman French
    6, 12, 27, 34, 52,
    59, 60

O
old dog new tricks 123
once bitten, twice shy 82

P
pariah dog 74–75
Pavlov's dog 71
pinscher 41
pooch 10
poodle 66–67
poodle-fakers 67
prairie dog 74
Puck 10
pug 10
pup, puppy 22
putting on the dog 84

R
raining cats and dogs
    110–111
Reagan, Ronald 20
Rex 21
Rosa canina 38
Rottweiler 40
Rover 35
run away with his tail
    between his legs
    83, 101

Acknowledgments & credits

Ivy Press would like to thank Penny Hamill of Beltinge Bassets, Herne Bay, Kent, U.K. for her time and assistance, and her Basset Hound Marvin for being such a star.

PRONUNCIATION

The guide to pronunciation provided throughout "Doggy Words" is a simple system based on respelling. For more information, please see *Universal Dictionary* by Reader's Digest.

PHOTO CREDITS

The publisher wishes to thank the following for the use of pictures:

Linda Bucklin/iStockphoto: plane, p.14

Sergei Popov/iStockphoto: palm, p.86

Jupiter Images: for all other images accompanying Professor Marvin

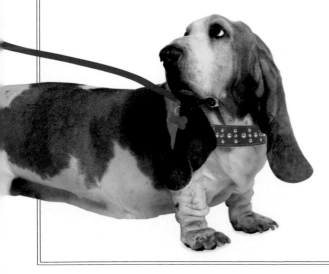